My Life

My Life
Transformed By Parkinson's Disease

LIVING WITH A CHRONIC ILLNESS
(A PERSONAL ACCOUNT)
BY
CHARLES P. ATTERBURY

My Life Transformed by Charles P. Atterbury

This book is written to provide information and motivation to readers. Its purpose is not to render any type of psychological, legal, or professional advice of any kind. The content is the sole opinion and expression of the author, and not necessarily that of the publisher.

Copyright © 2018 by Charles P. Atterbury

All rights reserved. No part of this book may be reproduced, transmitted, or distributed in any form by any means, including, but not limited to, recording, photocopying, or taking screenshots of parts of the book, without prior written permission from the author or the publisher. Brief quotations for noncommercial purposes, such as book reviews, permitted by Fair Use of the U.S. Copyright Law, are allowed without written permissions, as long as such quotations do not cause damage to the book's commercial value. For permissions, write to the publisher, whose address is stated below.

Printed in the United States of America.

ISBN   978-1-949746-24-2   (Paperback)
ISBN   978-1-949746-25-9   (Digital)

Lettra Press books may be ordered through booksellers or by contacting:

Lettra Press LLC
18229 E 52nd Ave.
Denver City, CO 80249
1 303-586-1431 | info@lettrapress.com
www.lettrapress.com

Contents

What Is Parkinson's Disease..1

Life Before Parkinson's

Early Beginings 7
Growing Up 9
Elementary Years...11
High School Years...13
Being Responsible...15

Young Adulthood

Creating Excitement...21
Being The Nucleus... 22
Being Adventurous..23
Always Assisting... 28
Reliable 29
Funny 30
Providing Moral Support 32
Mischievous...33
Full Of Anxiety 34

As An Adult

Overseas Travelling Experiences 38
Parenthood..45
Challenges And Rewards- Growing Up In A Large Family.......... 48
Coming To America...53

Summary	55
A Visit To My Doctor	56
Experience At The Diagnostic Center	58
Treatment At Rockland Neurological	60
Treatment At Columbia	67
Brain Surgery	74
After The Surgery	76
Convalescence	78
Return To Active Duty	80
Living With Parkinson's	81

What Is Parkinson's Disease

The Parkinson's Center of Oregon, located at Oregon Health & Science University, defines Parkinson's disease and describes the symptoms and appearance as follows:

Parkinson's disease is a progressive degenerative neurological disorder affecting the region of the brain known as the *substantia nigra* that manufactures the chemical *dopamine* necessary for controlling movement and fine motor skills. The most common symptoms are tremor, muscular stiffness, and slowness of movement. While experts agree symptoms are due to a deficiency of the brain chemical, dopamine, they are uncertain as to why the nerve cells containing dopamine die. Parkinsons is not contagious.

SYMTOMS AND APPEARANCE

The Parkinson's Center of Oregon, located at Oregon Health & Science University, defines Parkinson's disease and describes the symptoms and appearance as follows:

Slowness of movement

This is the most disabling symptom. Initially, it often begins in one arm with a loss of manual dexterity. The slowness makes it difficult to get out of a chair or turn in bed. Fine movements such as buttoning clothing, handwriting, and using a fork or knife may become difficult.

Later, the person appears to be in slow motion and if not treated may become virtually frozen like a statue. Because of the enormous energy it takes to overcome slowness the person with Parkinson's often complains of being "weak" although there is not true muscular weakness.

Tremor

Tremor occurs in about two-thirds of people with Parkinson's and is often the most visible and obvious sign of the disease. While the Parkinson's tremor usually affects the hands and feet it sometimes involves the lips, tongue, and jaw. The tremor is more visible while at rest or while walking and will usually stop during movement of the hand.

Muscle stiffness

Stiffness combined with slowness may cause aching muscles and joints, especially in the shoulders. This is sometimes misinterpreted as "arthritis" or "bursitis".

Masked face

An often confusing characteristic of the disease is the presence of a "masked face" showing little or no emotion. Blinking and spontaneous eye movements are less frequent, giving rise to a staring expression. This can be misinterpreted as lack of interest or depression.

Walking difficulties

The gait may be slow with short steps. A person with Parkinson's may also intermittently freeze as if the feet were stuck to the floor. Freezing occurs especially when approaching doorways or if forced to hurry. There is a propensity to bend the trunk forward and to walk without swinging the arms. It is common to have difficulties with balance.

Speech problems

About one half of all individuals with Parkinson's disease develop difficulty with their speech. The most common problem is a soft or fading voice. Communication can be complicated further by a fast mumbling speech with uncontrollable repetitions of the first syllable.

Swallowing difficulties

Some individuals experience difficulty eating because their ability to swallow has become impaired. Food may collect in the mouth or the back of the throat resulting in choking or coughing.

Troubling inconsistencies

It is very important to note that an individual's symptoms may vary from Moment-to-Moment and day-to-day. Symptoms may be nonexistent one minute only to suddenly reappear for no clear reason.[1]

The Parkinson's Center of Oregon also advises that although there are different types of parkinsonism, the most common condition today is the one first recognized in 1817 by James Parkinson the British physician who first described the symptoms in a published article that he called "The shaking palsy". The disease is both chronic and progressive. This means that it lasts over a long time period and the symptoms worsen as time goes by. It is Idiopathic, which means there is no known cause. Generally it affects people over 60 years old, and it is more common in men than in women. The incidence of Parkinsons disease increases with age and is uncommon in people younger than forty. Although it is not a regular feature, intellectual impairment may occasionally occur in the later stages of the disease.

The Parkinson's Center of Oregon further states that Parkinsons disease affects both men and women across all ethnic lines. An estimated 1,500,000 people in the United States are afflicted with this disease.

Presently there is no cure for PARKINSON'S but there are drugs that may be used to retard its progress, especially in the early stages. Also, there are medical procedures currently in use to control the tremors associated with this disease.

Among some notable people that have been diagnosed with PARKINSON'S are Mohammed Ali, former heavyweight boxing champion; Janet Reno, former U.S. Attorney General; and Michael J. Fox, film star.

---

[1] <http://www.ohsu.edu/som-neuro/parkinsons/parkinsons.html>

Life Before Parkinson's

Early Beginings

I was born in Brown's Town in the parish of St. Ann on the Island of Jamaica West Indies on February 20th 1954. I am the first of my parents' six children. My family members and close friends know me as Max. There are two younger sisters: Andrea, affectionately known as Val, and Dorothea, whom we call Beth. My younger brothers are Peter, Osmond (Pat) and John. They follow me in the same order as their names are listed. There are three older siblings alive from my Father's previous relationships: Gloria, Grace and Barbara. An older brother Karl is deceased. My Father worked for the Jamaican Government as a public health inspector and when we were young children, he was transferred to the neighboring parish to the east, St. Mary, to be the Chief Public Health Inspector for that parish. We actually grew up in St. Mary. Of my younger siblings, John was the only one not born in St. Ann.

During the week preceding August 6^{th,} 1962, the day Jamaica commemorated its independence from England, my Father relocated us all to the Village of Galina in St. Mary. There were notable differences between the house we lived in Brown's Town and the one we were going to live at in Galina. The soil in Galina had a natural color whereas the soil in Brown's Town was red, due to the existence of bauxite in it, from which aluminum is extracted. The house in Galina was along the main road for all traffic heading to Port Maria, the capital of St. Mary; whereas the Brown's Town house was secluded. There was much more playing area in Galina. We had neighbors to our left and an open lot to the right where some boys used to play cricket. There were three children in the house next door and we soon became close friends. There were lots of hills behind the house and we took great pleasure in climbing them. It was a new adventure.

One day during our climb we came across an open cave. When we returned to the house we excitedly told our mother about it. This was during the summer and my mother used this as an opportunity to get us out the house during the days by preparing lunches for all of us, placing them in a basket and telling us to return in time to get washed up for the evening before our father came home from work.

M<y mother was a primary school teacher so she was very strict with us. If she told you not to touch something and you disobeyed her she would hit you on the fingers. We used to have fun with her because if she wanted one of us she would call every body's name before she called the one she really wanted.

My father's office was located in Port Maria, so we went to the Port Maria Primary School for elementary education where my mother was also a teacher. We were taken to and from school by Dad. The children next door also went to the same school, and their mother was a teacher there too.

Our parents taught us not to get in fights at school-to walk away if anybody hit us. When I attended the primary school I used to be bullied because I was new to the other boys who knew each other for a long time. One day while one of the boys was bullying me I lost my composure and retaliated leaving him in a heap. From that day forward nobody else picked on me. I was the protector for my brothers and sisters and would shield them from anybody who would try to hurt them. Pat kept me the busiest, because he always picked on boys sometimes twice his size then he would run to me for protection.

Whenever things needed to be repaired around the house my Father would get a repair man to fix them. I would observe him while he was repairing the problem frequently asking why things were done in a particular way. In the future if this same problem surfaced I was the repair man.

In 1966, my Father bought a house about 1 mile west of the Galina house in a district called Wilderness in front of the ocean. The name of the property is "Rockhind" which is an apt description of what the land was like. John my youngest brother still resides there.

Growing Up

Many of my family members and close friends will tell you that I was very active when I was much younger. I enjoyed being a handyman and it gave me some feeling of accomplishment and fulfillment looking at the end result. I was always the first to offer to fix anything that needed repairing, as long as it was within my capabilities and I had the right tools. Being the firstborn I was taught that my behavior and actions should be above reproach so that my younger siblings would look up to me for setting the standard which they were to follow. You can just imagine the pressure I felt and placed upon myself thinking that everything I did had to be right and perfect. I used to be so critical about the things my brothers and sisters did that it earned me the dubious distinction of being called "Mr. Perfect" or "Mr. P" as my younger sister Beth would call me.

As a child I enjoyed playing with my siblings. We formed our own teams challenging each other in games like cricket, baseball, football (soccer), and track and field events. When I graduated from high school it gave me great pleasure transporting them to school so they would not have to take the bus. When we had all left school you could see us together at parties and other social events. Of course there was a midnight house curfew which we frequently broke provoking the ire of our parents. Soon after I started working I opened up their first bank accounts.

We had many fruit trees on the property: several varieties of mangoes, almonds, oranges, coconuts, grapefruits, pineapples, guava, limes, tamarind, banana and plantain. You name it and we probably had it at home. The boys used to climb most of these fruit trees and eat the fruit from the branches, while filling bags with the fruit for our parents and sisters. On some Sundays after church service my

Father would pick some young coconuts (jelly coconuts), cut open the tops so we drank the water inside, and then slit them open with a machete for us to eat the "jelly"(or as we called it the meat) with a spoon or with one improvised from the coconut husk. Nothing could compare with my Father picking oranges from the tree early in the morning with the dew on them. It was as if the orange had just been removed from the refrigerator, very cold and refreshing.

Of course, we all had our chores to do around the house. Every one of us had an assigned day for working in the kitchen with Mom. My day was Monday. On Saturdays all the boys had kitchen duty, and on Sundays it was time for the girls. This means that you learnt how to cook and were responsible for washing the dishes and scouring the pots after meals. In addition, we were responsible for cleaning our own bedrooms and other designated sections of the house. The responsibility for raking the leaves in the yard on Saturdays was shared amongst the boys.

On Sundays it was church three times for the day. First, there was the morning service at 7:00 on the 1st and 3rd Sundays of each month when there was Holy Communion administered by the priest, or at 9:00 on the 2nd and 4th Sundays for regular service, which was led by a lay preacher. Sunday school was at 4:00pm and night service at 7:00. It was mandatory for us to attend all the services, since my mother played the organ and my father was the preacher sometimes. I was an altar boy and carried the cross.

When we lived in Galina, but before we started to attend high school, my parents had three close friends who were also active in their churches. Every Christmas morning after all our church services were over, we would move from each other's house until about midday celebrating the joys of the season. Then we would return to our own houses to celebrate with our respective families.

Elementary Years

During my elementary school years, I was a Cub Scout and used to go for hikes and attend weekend camps. We were taught how to cook, the correct way to make a bed, the art of sewing and how to use a rope to make various types of knots. Maybe one of the reasons I enjoy jumble words and crossword puzzles is that during the summer holidays, Mom gave us copies of these puzzles from the daily newspaper which had to be solved before lunch time. If they were incomplete we were not allowed to play until my mother was satisfied that we had tried our best. This practice forced us to read anything (books and periodicals) something she could not get us to do otherwise, in order to learn new words.

I can recall the year that President Kennedy was assassinated, I was attending primary school. One of the grounds men from the school was on the street running an errand when he heard the news on the radio. On his return to the school, he made the announcement by shouting at the top of his voice for everybody to hear that President Kennedy was shot and killed in Dallas. When it actually sank in that the president of the U.S. was dead the entire school took on a somber appearance.

In order to attend the high school we had to pass the Common Entrance Examinations testing annually which was administered by the Ministry of Education on the last Friday in January if you were at least eleven years old. The results were usually published in the daily newspaper just about the time schools were closing for the summer holidays. The highest award was for a full government scholarship whereby you were sent to a boarding school usually an elite one, where the government paid for accommodations, tuition and the cost of books. The next level was a regular government scholarship, where

Charles P. Atterbury

the cost of tuition and books were paid by the government. Following this were the free place winners, where tuition was free but you had to pay for the books. Finally there were the fee paying students who had to pay their own tuition and purchase their books. I went to high school as a free place winner.

High School Years

While attending high school, I was an army cadet and took great pleasure in keeping my uniform neat and tidy. I loved to shine the boots using a candle to burn the heels and toes, then using water and shoe polish to give it the sheen. Keeping the brass shined was a challenge because some of the items were small. Nevertheless I enjoyed doing it because you were always competing with fellow cadets to see whose items came out the shiniest. I was heavily involved in sports. The school was divided into four Houses. On the day of registration each student was assigned to a House based on the first letter of the last name. I was even nominated to be the House Captain for one school year. These sporting activities included cricket, football (soccer), track and field and table tennis (ping pong). In my senior year I had the privilege of driving the family car to school because my father was working overseas and Mom could not drive.

One Friday morning the Commanding Officer for the Cadets, who was also a student, did an inventory of uniforms and supplies when he discovered that we were short of many things. The only way to replace these items was to pick them up from the Army Headquarters which was some thirty miles away in Kingston. We needed them as early as possible because we were due for an annual inspection. I volunteered to drive us to Kingston if we could get enough money to purchase gas. No time was wasted finding the money for the gas so we headed for the nearest gas station fueled up and headed for Kingston without telling anyone.

Our plan was to drive to Army Headquarters collect the items that we needed and return to school before dismissal. We got there in good time picked up the stuff and were on our return journey to the school. On our way back we saw a car approaching us from the opposite direction. The closer we got to it the more familiar it appeared to be. **It was the headmaster for our school.** Upon recognizing the car everybody ducked and I was the only one who could not hide. He was going home for the weekend to Kingston where he had his house. During the week he lived in a rented house near to the school. We got back on campus without any further incidents and before school was dismissed for the day.

The following Monday morning I was summoned by the headmaster to his office. On the way there I feared the worst like being suspended or being caned. When I arrived at his office, he asked me if that was my car he passed on Friday afternoon on his way home and wanted to know where I was coming from. I answered in the affirmative then went on to explain that we had gone to the Army Headquarters to pick up some supplies which we desperately needed for the upcoming annual inspection. He then sent for the Commanding Officer to verify my story. After satisfying himself that I was telling the truth he advised us that in the future such an errand should not be performed without the school's approval. With that we were dismissed and I felt very relieved.

Being Responsible

When my Father retired from the government services, he worked on a contract for the government of the Cayman Islands as the Chief Health Inspector and lived in Grand Cayman the largest of the three islands. Being the only other person in the household with a driver's license, I had the **responsibility** of transporting my family anywhere and everywhere that we had to go. From these experiences I developed the love of driving. I taught most of my younger siblings and my mother how to drive. Driving was a passion and I enjoyed transporting people wherever they needed to go as long as I was available.

It was very interesting teaching each one to drive. We had to literally force Peter to drive because he was so lazy but he was good at it. When he went for the driving test he passed it on the first attempt. As it turned out he proved to be the best and fastest driver in the family. It was more difficult to teach Pat to drive because of his erratic behavior. He got his driver's license on the second attempt. My mother was a classic. She had a phobia for heights. If she was travelling in any vehicle you could not get her to look over her shoulder once the car was ascending a hill and there was nothing to block her view from looking down the precipice. If she was talking she would suddenly become silent. So it was no surprise when learning how to drive she would stop the car midway on a hill and tell me to take over. It took all three of us older boys to coax her into believing that everything would be all right. She must have set the record for number of attempts to pass the driving test. Of my two younger sisters Beth was more interested. I remember teaching her to reverse one day using the hedge in the front of the yard as her guide. She started out ok, but somewhere between the middle and the end of the hedge she lost her focus and drove the car along it for the rest of the way. When she came out of the car she was very apologetic so I comforted her by saying that all will be fine that the car is only scratched. She never gave up and went on to get her driver's license.

During the time that my father was working overseas and we were teenagers, the house was being renovated. My mother therefore had to oversea the workmen. Possibly because she was a woman, the workmen started to take advantage of her: getting her to purchase unnecessary building materials and charging her for work never done. She was afraid the money for the construction would be spent before the house was finished.

Seeing her frustration and the advantage taken because our father was not there, we had a "children's meeting" to determine what we could do to ease the burden. It was decided that we had observed the manner in which the workmen performed certain jobs and that if we were careful we could do the job just as well. We decided amongst ourselves that our father had all the tools that were needed to complete the job. With our course of action in hand it was time to approach our mother with our plan.

A family meeting was convened and we point blank told Mom to get rid of the workmen. Of course if you know my mother, she wanted to know how the renovation of the house would be completed. Looking at each other we said that it would be done by the six of us children. We further let her know that by observing what each tradesman did we could do it just as well and we were tired of seeing her being abused by these workmen. Furthermore she could save on the money she would be paying out for labor expenses. All this was taking place during the school year and being a teacher, she wanted to know how we would fit in our school work with such a major undertaking. We advised her that we would do the easier things on the week days and the major things on weekends. Tools would not be a problem because our father who was very handy around the house had all the tools that we needed. Reluctantly she agreed. It was now up to her to sell our case to dad.

When she spoke to dad she explained everything to him the way we had done to her. As usual my dad asked mom what she thought about it. She let him know how adamant we were in completing the job. He thought it over for awhile and quietly gave his approval.

Mom got rid of the workmen. Now it was up to us to put our money where our mouths were. Each of us had a specific task and we set out to finish the construction. It took us about two weeks to complete the major tasks such as installing windows, tiling a bathroom wall and installing lighting fixtures. The more refined things such as painting the walls were done in our own time. When we were finished Mom marveled at the hidden talents that we all possessed. On Dad's next visit home he was very impressed with our ingenuity.

During one of my father's visits while the house was being renovated, he decided we should clean up the yard because construction materials were scattered all over the place. The items that were reusable we put in one pile and the rest was placed on another pile to be burnt. The day was calm and Dad thought that it was ok to set the pile of garbage afire so he lit it. We all waited until there was no smoke emanating from the pile before we went into the house.

Later that evening I went out to visit a friend. When I returned later that night I saw a huge fire in the spot where we burnt the garbage earlier. We always had the garden hose attached to the water pipe in the front of the house: so I quickly stopped the car, headed for the hose, turned on the pipe, and then advanced towards the fire with the water running from the hose.

In my excitement I left the headlights of the car on and the engine running. With the commotion outside car headlights on and the motor running it awakened my parents.

When Dad came out and saw the blaze he was very jittery. He said that the garden hose could not provide enough pressure to quench the fire. We had no telephone to call the nearest fire station which was five miles away in Port Maria. This meant somebody had to drive to the fire station. My father suggested that I drive to the fire station and get the firemen. I suggested that he should go while I continue to fight the fire. In less than no time my Father took off.

Charles P. Atterbury

As I previously mentioned the family house is located opposite the ocean and during the late nights to early mornings there is a breeze from the sea which can be very high sometimes. This was one of those nights. When we thought the fire was put out earlier, apparently there were some embers which were fuelled by the high breeze from the ocean during the night. I kept on trying to keep the outer edges of the fire wet to prevent it from spreading any further. By this time the rest of the family was up trying to fill whatever containers they could find with water to throw on the fire.

Dad must have driven like a mad man because in what appeared to be about a half an hour after he left, I could hear a siren in the distance. As the sound got louder I became more anxious because I was not sure how much longer I could hold the fire at bay with the garden hose. Shortly afterwards the fire engine pulled up into the driveway and the firemen quickly got into action. In what appeared to be the twinkling of an eye the fire was extinguished.

After the firemen left my parents hugged me and thanked me for my quick reaction. No mention was made about the time I got home. It was one of those rare occasions the curfew was broken and was overlooked by them. Who knows what would have happened if I did not arrive home at that time?

Young Adulthood

Creating Excitement

As a young adult I created my share of **excitement** for the family. On one occasion it was the aftermath of a send-off party for my supervisor who was being promoted and transferred to another location. When the party was over some of the staff members had to be driven to their homes a little distance away. I readily volunteered to take them home because of my passion to drive. Everybody enquired if I was ok to drive considering that I had been driving for the job earlier that day. After reassuring them that I was all right and someone volunteered to accompany me for the return trip, I was allowed to drive.

I reached the destination safely. On my return journey I must have dozed off because I could not recall passing certain landmarks. **Then a bridge came in the path of the car.** Luckily the accident occurred close to the home of the person we held the party for. The person who accompanied me ran to the house to get him to come to the scene of the accident. I must have been unconscious because I cannot recall anything about the car hitting the bridge. I was told that the car had to be ripped apart so that my legs could be freed. Can you imagine my Mother visiting her firstborn in the hospital as a result of a motor vehicle accident on the morning of her birthday? I must have given my Mom the worst present a parent ever received on her birthday.

Then there was another incident when a family friend was visiting from overseas. For the weekend we decided to visit a very popular beach which is also a tourist attraction, to let loose. After selecting our spot on the beach we all went in for a swim. I accepted a challenge to swim to a reef in the water. Apparently I underestimated the distance ran into difficulties and had to be rescued by a lifeguard. YES, I almost drowned in front of my entire family.

As soon as I was resuscitated and had recovered enough we left for home. It was a dull end to a bright sunny day.

Being The Nucleus

Being **the nucleus** of most activities between my late teenage years and young adulthood could be attributed to the way my three best friends and I formed our relationship, which has been going on for approximately forty years. Even though we may not talk to or see each other as often as we used to, we are always aware of and keep abreast of each other's activities and reminisce about our wild days together whenever we meet. We try to call each other on our birthdays and during the Christmas holidays.

Three of us worked for the same company. I was fortunate to have the opportunity to travel around the country as a relieving officer. That was how I met my friends Ralston (whom we call Pess) and Wade (whom we call Buck), by doing relief assignments in the offices that they were working. Both of their aliases are abbreviations of their last names. As fate would have it, our company sent us on a scholarship that same year to a college in Kingston. I met my third "partner in crime" Dane, on the day I went to register for my classes. He was also on a scholarship from his company to do the same course as the rest of us.

On the first day of classes Pess, Buck and I sat together. Dane, who remembered our previous encounter when we were registering for classes, asked if he could join us. After classes that day, we formally introduced ourselves to each other. As the school year progressed we would learn the similarities among us. Two of us were born in the same year; two of us shared the same astrological sign; two of us were from large families; and two of us had parents who worked for the government services. I was the only one who fell in all these categories. By the end of the first semester we formed such a bond that even to this day it is still unbroken. We formed an alliance with each other.

Being Adventurous

Adventure was never lacking in my life. One weekend my three best friends and I embarked on a mission to see if we could drive through all fourteen parishes in the country, and visit some of the tourist attractions along the way.

Since we all grew up in different parts of the island, it would not be necessary for us to pay for overnight accommodations. The plan was for us to leave from Dane's parents' house in Kingston, spend the first night at my parents' house in St. Mary, since it was the most easterly parish, and then we would spend Saturday night at Pess's parents' house located in Trelawny to the western side of the island. On Sunday on our way back home, we planned to have dinner at Buck's parents' house in Manchester located on the south central part of the island.

We commenced our adventure from Dane's parents' house in Kingston at about 3:00pm, after we had something to eat on the Friday that classes were over for the semester. We travelled northwards for about twenty miles and stopped at our first tourist attraction, a Botanical Garden in St. Mary. We refused the offer of a guided tour and went aimlessly through the gardens. We stopped by a river that runs through the gardens and tried to catch some fish, unsuccessfully of course. After making fools of ourselves we resumed our journey westwards. Our next stop was at my parents' house. I introduced my friends to my mother and other family members. Then it was dinnertime. After eating dinner we chatted for awhile until it was time to retire for the night. Here we had my mother in stitches while we were deciding who would share beds, because this was the first time that we had to share accommodations, as we had never gone anywhere together where we had to stay overnight.

Charles P. Atterbury

After much debating it was decided that Dane and I would sleep on the same bed and Pess and Buck would share beds. With that issue finally resolved we turned in for the night. At this point we covered the parishes of Kingston, St. Andrew and St. Mary. With three parishes completed, we had eleven more to go.

We surfaced rather late on Saturday morning. My mother asked us why we got up at that time considering we had a lot of ground to cover. We told her we were very tired. After eating a hearty breakfast we bade her farewell and we set out on our way.

Still going westwards we stopped at another tourist attraction, "The Green Grotto Caves" in St. Ann. These are some caves in the Limestone area of the Island featuring an underground lake. After paying the entrance fees we were led by a tour guide who explained the features of the attraction. There were lots of stalactites and stalagmites, which are deposits of limestone looking like large icicles hanging from the ceiling or rising from the floor respectively. The highlight of this tour was to get in a boat for a ride on the underground lake. While we were touring the caves our group included four female American tourists. When we arrived at the location where the ride on the lake was scheduled to commence, we were looking for a boat; but what we saw was a dinghy which could not accommodate all of us. The guide told us that we would have to break up in two groups of four since the capacity on the "boat" was for four passengers plus himself. We decided amongst ourselves that our two groups of four would each comprise two men and two women. Dane and I decided to go first. Boarding of the vessel had to be done with precision. The tour guide was the first to get on and then we entered one at a time and stood towards the center of it. He cautioned us that if we converged too much on one side this could cause the vessel to capsize.

He pushed off from the "shore line" and our ride commenced. He informed us that the water was very clear from the limestone, we could even see the bottom and its deepest point was eleven feet. The lake was at the bottom of a cave and all our sounds were being echoed. When we returned and alighted from the vessel Pess and Buck boarded along with the two other women. When one of the women entered the vessel it tilted and she held onto Buck for support.

He politely advised she was making the wrong choice because he was a no swimmer and would not be able to help her if the boat capsized. We all started to laugh vehemently not so much about what he said but in the manner in which he said it. For the entire ride my friend held onto the vessel for dear life. When the vessel came back to "port" my friend gingerly got out. We spent about two hours at this stop then we resumed our journey still proceeding westwards.

Along the way to Pess's parent's house we stopped at a roadside food stall where we ate fish and then moved on. We converged on his parent's house just as it was getting dusk. After the introductions one of his brothers' informed us that he was going to take us to a party later that night. Hearing this changed our whole mood for the night because we had been feeling very tired. We had dinner, showered, put on some party clothes and we were gone in no time.

At the party our tiredness caught up with us. We went to sleep anywhere that we could find a comfortable spot. We marveled at how comfortably Dane was sleeping on a concrete ledge no more than 12 inches wide. Shortly afterwards we left the party for Pess's home so we could stretch out and get a more comfortable rest.

When we got to our friend's house there was no discussion about bed sharing since it was decided that we would be as we were the night before. At this point we were five parishes down, nine more to go.

We got up rather early on Sunday morning and after a brief breakfast, we headed out once more going west. We drove through the parish of St. James. Our next stop was at a beach in Hanover, where we changed into our bathing trunks and jumped into the water for a swim. Dane decided that he was going to teach Buck how to swim. The beach was marked off with a buoy so we lined up by the rope and took turns diving over the rope. The highlight of this stop was when it was my turn to dive over the rope. I lost my bathing trunks once I jumped up from the water so that when I dove over the rope it was a *Kodak Moment*. With time against us we quickly got dressed and hurriedly left the beach to resume our journey.

Heading now in an easterly direction, we drove through the parishes of Westmoreland and St. Elizabeth, with only brief stops for refreshments. We arrived at Buck's parents' home in Manchester at about 3:00pm. We did not need any introductions since we had met his family before. After a sumptuous meal we all passed out on the lawn.

We were awakened by his mother when it was getting too late. We got ourselves together and were shortly on our way. We had now completed ten parishes.

On our way back to Kingston we drove non-stop to our starting point passing through the parishes of Clarendon and St. Catherine. We arrived at Dane's parents' home at about 10:00pm. After a brief post trip discussion we departed for our respective homes, not before conceding that we fell short of our goal by missing to get to the two most easterly parishes of St. Thomas and Portland. Mission not accomplished.

We attended each other's weddings. The first to go was Dane. We had so much in common: being born under the same astrological sign, wives sharing the same astrological sign, both wives being their parents' youngest children. Our weddings were less than one month apart.

I married my high school sweetheart in St. Mary on January 7, 1978. As a part of the wedding package, the hotel providing the reception gave us a complimentary room. My friends somehow found out the location of our room and rented their rooms above and beside ours. During the night they started pounding on the walls and floors preventing us from sleeping. Additionally, Dane embarrassed his wife by running out of his hotel room in his birthday suit early the following morning startling the female hotel manager while she was doing her morning rounds.

Buck was the third to go because he could no longer wait on Pess. Our original plan was to get married in order of our ages. His was an incident-free affair and we all had a good time.

Finally it was time for Pess to take the bold step. Now this was the most interesting of all the weddings. The night before the ceremony he and Buck slept in my house in Bridgeport, which is a suburb of Kingston. The three of us had some liquid refreshments until way past midnight. The ceremony was scheduled for 10:00am the following day which was a Saturday.

We woke up and found Pess on the floor and he could not explain how he ended up there. After we all showered and got dressed, we left for Kingston where the ceremony was to take place. It was an outdoor setting located in a garden. Upon our arrival the person who was officiating asked us if we realized that we were two hours late. We looked at each other embarrassed because his fiancée was already there waiting for him. When it was time for him to take the marriage vows he could not for the life of him remember the name of his fiancée and stumbled on it because he was so nervous. The minister smiled and said, "Whatever" and proceeded with the rest of the ceremony.

When it was over we all had a good laugh and teased him about not being able to remember his wife's name on the most important day of their lives.

Always Assisting

I was always **willing to assist.** I was working in Buck's parish at his office in Manchester. (We were not yet friends). Seated on the hotel patio one day after work I saw a lady having problems with her car. I quickly went out to help her. It would later turn out that she was Buck's Mother.

On another occasion I was taking my mother and one of her friends to go shopping in Kingston. Along the way somewhere in the distance I noticed that two cars were involved in a traffic accident. The closer I got to the scene the more I recognized one of the cars involved. It belonged to my aunt my mother's oldest sister. The other driver appeared to be at fault but was having the upper hand of my aunt and her husband. I quickly pulled up, jumped from my car and started defending my aunt and uncle. There was a Police Station a short distance away and I knew the traffic cop assigned there. I told my mother to stay with her sister while I went to get the cop. When he arrived on the scene and had things under control I resumed my journey. On the way my mother expressed how surprised she was at my actions but proud of the way I took control of the accident as my aunt and uncle appeared to be defenseless.

Reliable

My parents could always **rely on me.** One Saturday morning my father woke up very early and got dressed to attend the funeral service for one of his good friends. Now he no longer drove so there were no cars at home and my mother was not aware of any transportation arrangements to take him to the funeral. My mother asked him how he was going to get there. He politely told her that once I found out about his friend's death I would come to take him to the funeral.

Earlier in the week I did see the death announcement of my father's friend and had a hunch he would want to attend the funeral. Not being able to contact him by phone, I got up very early that Saturday morning, left Kingston and travelled to my parents' house. When I arrived Dad was seated in his favorite chair on the verandah reading the daily newspaper. I told Dad I had seen his friend's death announcement in the newspaper, assumed he would want to attend the funeral, and decided to drive home so I could take him. His face lit up when heard this. He knew that once I heard about the death of his friend I would be there to take him to the funeral. He then turned to my mother and said "See I told you that once he found out about the funeral, he would be coming to take me there."

Before Dad retired, Mom used to go to the open market on Saturdays, and we each took turns to accompany her. When Dad left to work overseas, I had the responsibility of taking her there. On the odd occasion that she could not make it, I did the shopping from a list that she gave me. What was interesting about shopping with my mother was that she had a special higgler (haggler) for certain items even though she could get most things from any one of them.

Funny

I mentioned earlier that my father worked on contract for the Cayman Islands government, but did I mention that I was **funny?** When his contract was about to expire, he realized he had a lot of personal belongings he wanted to bring home, but they were too numerous for him handle by himself. At that time Buck had never travelled on an airplane; so I told him about my father's plight. We decided that this would be the opportunity for him to experience his first plane ride and we could take back some of my father's belongings. I had visited my father previously so this would not be my first plane ride. We arranged to take a one week vacation together so we could visit my Dad.

The day finally came and we were met by Dad at the airport. During the ride to his house we brought him up to date on the happenings back home. When we arrived at his house he smiled and advised us that each of us could have his own bedroom because it was a three bedroom house. My Mother had filled him in about the weekend episode at our house with my friends.

During the days while Dad worked, we used his car to visit tourist attractions, shopping areas and the beaches. One day we decided to go to the movies. It was the most disorganized seating arrangement we had ever seen. We could not sit beside each other because people who came as a group spread out all over the hall. During the movie *Smokey and the Bandit*, we kept shouting to each other every time there was a humorous scene. We were never so impatient to leave a movie to discuss the funny scenes.

On the night before we left and while we were packing, my father observed that we had some fruit that would not clear customs at the airport back home. At that time it was considered contraband.

We insisted that we were going to take them with us. At this point he asked us what we would do if they disallowed them to enter the country. We told him that we would eat them because that's what the customs officers do when food items were confiscated. Dad said it was a lot to eat. Then we told him that his house was five minutes from the airport and the plane flies over it, so when we see the plane flying over his house we will go to the bathroom and clear the way for what may come when we get home. On the day that we were leaving, as soon as the plane passed overhead we headed for the bathrooms. My Dad cracked up because he did not take us seriously at first.

Imagine, after going through all of that preparation the customs officers allowed us to take the fruit with us.

Providing Moral Support

As for giving **moral support** I could always be relied upon. My friend Pess operates a security company that provides armed guards, watch dogs and foot patrolmen with locations throughout the island. We always met at his office on Friday evenings to review our weekly activities and then to go out for a few drinks. One particular Friday when I arrived at his office he had a very somber look. I was very concerned because among the group of us four he was the one who was always laughing. Then I learned that one of his guards was shot and killed at a location in one of the rural parts of the country. I offered to take him there if it would help to set his mind at ease. He said that he would not mind. I took him to the site.

Mischievous

My friends and I were never short in **the mischief** department. One pay day while we were students we went to a restaurant to treat ourselves to a decent meal. We sat together and the waiter passed our table no less than six times to take other customers orders. We started to voice our dissatisfaction about not being acknowledged. The manager heard our complaints and came over to apologize. Shortly thereafter the waiter came over and took our orders. We waited until he served the meals and then we got up and left the restaurant without eating or paying for the food.

On another occasion we were driving from classes in separate cars when another driver pulled out suddenly from a side street in front of Dane's car. By the time he applied the brakes it was too late and he bumped into the other car. We all pulled over. While we were trying to settle who was at fault, the other driver {who was from one of the rural areas) blurted out that he knew Bob Marley. Being upset by the whole incident we let him know what he should do with Bob Marley.

Full Of Anxiety

Like many young people I dreamed of buying a new car, but my circumstance was a bit unusual. The first time I saw my car was the night I went to pick it up. **Yes I said *NIGHT*.** The whole transaction depended on my trusting the sales manager and him believing in me. The color and type of car that I wanted was only available from his dealership, which was located in Montego Bay in the western part of the island more than seventy miles from my home on the eastern end. Everything was done by phone with special emphasis made on the color which had to be RED.

On the day that I was to pick up my new car I was faced with a huge problem. My father was coming home to visit us during one of his officially paid trips allowable on his overseas contract. The airport was located in Kingston over fifty miles southeast of our home.

I anxiously called my father and explained my situation. He calmly responded by telling me to call the sales manager and to tell him I could only get the car after hours. I had to pick up my father at the airport! After listening to my plight, the sales manager promised to call me back with a solution. Not hearing from him within an hour, I started to get very fidgety on the job and had to be consoled by my boss. About two hours had elapsed when I received his call outlining the procedure to pick up the car. He would have the car registered and insured, and the keys would be at the security office. I was to bring a bank check to the security guard for the cost of the car plus the cost for the registration and insurance. As this was a Friday and the dealership was closed on the weekend, you can only imagine my fear that everything went smoothly. Excitedly I called my father with the resolution.

With my mother and some of my siblings I went to pick up my father after work that day. The flight was on time so we were in and out of Kingston in no time. We got home by 9:00pm. My Dad suggested that we rest for awhile. Phase one completed.

About an hour later my parents' and one of my brother's accompanied me to pick up my new car in Montego Bay. As the minutes ticked by the more petrified I became thinking about "what if" things did not go as planned. I had given my mother the check to hold for safe keeping and verified that she had it with her.

We arrived at the dealership which was surrounded by a high chain link fence at about 11:30pm. I pulled up to the front gate and honked the car horn to alert the guard that somebody was at the gate. By this time I observed that there was a red car separated from the other cars in the showroom, and it had registration plates attached. I nudged by brother who had accompanied us and excitedly said to him that must be my car. The security guard stealthily left his office and asked what I needed. Anxiously I told him who I was and the purpose of my visit. He then approached the gate and after verifying my identification, we accompanied him to his security office to complete the necessary paper work. My mother handed me the check which I then gave him in exchange for the keys to my BRAND NEW FORD ESCORT. Phase two completed.

For the return journey my father drove the family car accompanied by my mother, while my brother travelled with me. Before we **left for the ride back home my father cautioned me not to exceed 50 mph, as I had to gradually "break the** car in." He let me drive in front. The traffic on the way back home was extremely light. We pulled up in our driveway at about 2:30 am on Saturday. After that exhausting day we all retired to bed, being thankful to my father for taking me to pick up my car so soon after he had come home from overseas. I had to be at work at 8:00am. Final phase completed.

I was so anxious to see what the car looked like in daylight I do not think I slept much that night. It rained during the wee hours of the morning. By daylight I was up and was outside washing and admiring the car.

On Monday when I returned to work, I called the sales manager and expressed my gratitude to him for organizing to make things run so smoothly the previous Friday night.

As An Adult

When I lived on my own I did most of the minor repairs around the house; plumbing, electrical, painting and even gardening. I took great pride in the appearance of my yard. I spent a lot of time raking leaves and other debris from the lawn, watering the grass and removing weeds from the garden. Every Christmas I would repaint the house. My handiness was not limited to doing things at home. I did a lot of community activities through the service club that I was a member of. I did minor repairs to my car including brake repairs and tune-ups and spent a lot of time on the weekends to keep it clean and spotless. Whenever my friends passed through my neighborhood, they always stopped by my house for a *thirst-quencher* because I had a large assortment to choose from.

One Christmas morning while I was preparing breakfast somebody rapped on the front door. After investigating I realized it was Pess, so I let him in and soon realized that he was tipsy. He was on his way home after coming in from the rural area where he worked. We both ate and I offered to drive him home. He rejected my offer saying that he was OK. I decided to drive with him to keep him company and try to keep him awake. On the way we stopped at Dane's home. He offered us a *thirst-quencher* and I told him that Pess should not have any more. He insisted that he was all right and had one anyway. When it was time to leave I once more offered to drive him home again he refused. I pleaded with Dane to force him to let me do the driving. He told me that he would administer a sobriety test. He had Pess walk on a straight line of tiles then declared him fit to drive.

I nervously got in the car for the continuation of the ride to his house. He started out normally and then he began to drive erratically.

I started to coax him by telling him we were not in any hurry to get to his house. He slowed down for a while. Then the erratic driving restarted; again I was able to slow him down. I realized that if I kept talking to him he would drive calmly. When we were about three miles from his house I thought that he saw the rock, so I did not say anything to him. It felt like the world was turning upside down. The next Moment we were crawling through the top of the car. He hit the stone so hard that the car overturned and faced the opposite direction. After determining that we had no injuries and the only casualty was the car which had a dent on the top where it landed I cursed at him, got some help to upright the car, took the keys and drove the rest of the way to his house. When we got there we just went straight to bed.

As often as it was possible if I had nothing planned on some weekends it was off to the beach for a swim and picnic with family or friends.

Overseas Travelling Experiences

With the two jobs that I had in Jamaica **I travelled extensively**. One of them afforded me the opportunity to work overseas, a treat I usually looked forward to.

On one of these overseas assignments I went to work in Belize which shares its northern border with the south east of Mexico. As a youngster I was always challenged to learn new places. During the week I made several enquires about going to Mexico and found out that a bus goes to the town of Chetumal, the closest Mexican village to Belize. Being an **adventurous** person I made arrangements to cross the border on the weekend to visit that Mexican town and obtained the necessary documentation which was needed for the trip.

On that Saturday morning I got up very early and walked from my hotel to the bus station not far away. I was armed with my passport and an English/Spanish cheat card comprising the Spanish equivalent of popular English phrases, such as " good day"; " may I have something to eat"; " may I use the rest room"; " may I have a beer please"? I was very familiar with the last one because I loved my cerveza. On the way to Mexico the bus which was a regular commuter transporter, made frequent stops for people to get on or off from it. At one of these stops the bus stalled and it would not restart. The conductor announced that he would like all the men to get off the bus and give it a push. We all came off the bus and shoved it and shortly afterwards the bus engine roared into life again. We got back on and were once more on our way.

The next stop was a learning experience for me. I had never entered into another country by land; it was always by air because I am an "Island Guy". On the Belize side of the border we all got off the bus and had the Immigration officer issue us an exit pass. At the end of this process we all got back on the bus and the driver took off. He crossed a bridge and landed on Mexican soil. We had to leave the bus again to be processed by the Mexican Immigration officers. With this behind us, once more we boarded the bus where the driver took us to the bus terminal. Before we got off the bus the driver announced the departure time. When I glanced at my watch it only gave me about three hours to look around. I had travelled alone so I kept going back to the terminus to see if the bus was still there being a little anxious. To compound it all we arrived in Mexico during their siesta so the stores were all closed. This made me even more nervous about missing the bus to get back. Within ninety minutes the town was back to life. I tried doing a crash speed shopping expedition not venturing too far from the bus terminus and constantly checking my watch for the time.

I was cautioned before by the people in Belize, not to be fooled by the prices in pesos because upon conversion to the US dollar it could cost me more. The first store I approached I could not believe what I was seeing: appliances with sticker prices for 420,000.00 pesos, TV sets for 800,000.00 pesos and other astronomical prices. I had never seen so many zeros on a price tag anywhere before. After browsing through other stores for a while I decided to settle for a pair of Zapata's (shoes) costing 42,000.00 pesos (about US$15.00 at that time) for my son. Since the departure time for the bus was rapidly approaching, I hastened to the bus terminus and was one of the first people to return. Except for the immigration processes where we had to get off and re-board the bus, the return ride was incident free and uneventful. When I returned to the hotel I was just barely able to take a cold shower and have something to eat before I fell asleep for the night. It was an exhaustive day mentally and physically.

On another occasion I went to work on the Caribbean island of St. Lucia which has a dormant volcano. It is the only one in the world where people can actually walk through. As usual whenever I visit a foreign country I make arrangements to visit the points of interest on the weekends. There was no exception for this trip. A group of us rented a minivan that Saturday and due to the undulation of the roadways I was appointed the designated driver because of similar road conditions in Jamaica. Our first stop was at a lookout point by the Governor's mansion on the hills overlooking the capital Castries. It was very picturesque with many different colored boats and ships docked in the harbor and the general landscape was lush and green. After taking pictures of the scenery we proceeded with our tour. Next stop on our itinerary was at an old wine mill called "The Still". We just briefly looked around and then left as there was nothing that interested us there since the building appeared to be abandoned. We resumed our drive towards our feature attraction the site of the **Soufriere Volcano.** On our way we saw two mountain ranges side by side rising up from the sea. Then I recalled studying in my high school geography class about the twin Peaks, the Pitons of St. Lucia. The larger one is known as the **Gros Piton** and the smaller one **Petit Piton**. It was so amazing to actually see something that you studied in school about the geography of another country. We stopped and took pictures of the mountain ranges which just seemed to appear out of the water. With that behind us, we continued toward the main purpose of the excursion.

We arrived at Mt. Soufriere the site of the dormant volcano and secured a tour guide who would lead us through the volcano. He explained to us that because it is so open the gases are unable to build up enough pressure for it to erupt. He advised us that the bubbles we saw on either side of our pathway were sulphurus and the temperature can get up to about 300 degrees Fahrenheit. It was so hot I had already removed my shirt. When the guide looked and saw my watch and bracelet getting black he acknowledged that he had forgotten to advise us to remove all silver jewelry because the gas causes them to get black. I became concerned that my jewelry was damaged because of his omission. He calmly advised us that it would be taken care of at the end of the tour.

He then showed us a stream with what appeared to be black water and many people were bathing naked in it. He explained that the water had many minerals from the volcanic gases and fluids which flowed from the volcano and that by bathing in the water, people believed in the healing powers of the minerals which were good for joint pains and cleansing of the skin.

At the end of the tour he cleaned the jewelry with limestone which restored them to their former luster. This enabled us to allay all our fears of losing our prized possessions.

Parenthood

June 21st 1980 is a date that has left an indelible mark in my life. That was the day I witnessed the birth of my son Sheldon. He was such a chubby baby we used to call him "Shelly Belly", a name he no longer acknowledges or responds to.

As a father I enjoyed spending time with him. I remember one incident when he was about two years old I was servicing the car by applying grease to the front wheel bearings and adjusting the brakes. He was in the middle of all the activities. I had just put grease on one of the bearings and set it on the ground when he mischievously picked it up. I told him to return it to where he got it from. When he set it back on the ground and saw that his hands were black from the grease, he immediately wiped them on his shirt next they were on his face. He looked like a grease monkey by the time I was finished working on the car. He gave me such a good laugh just looking at him standing so innocently and bragging to his mother how he assisted me with the grease all over his body.

I remember teaching him to ride his bicycle. He would get very frustrated each time he lost his balance and fell off the bike hitting the ground. One day after he fell off the bicycle and was becoming annoyed I told him not to ride the bicycle if he did not want to fall. I explained to him that he had to learn to balance the bicycle by pedaling when he moved off. He never complained about falling again after those words of advice and he went on to become a very good cyclist.

Whenever I was not travelling for work, he always looked forward to me coming home so that we could watch TV together or play Mario on his Nintendo system in his bedroom. In me he found a beating stick because I could never move the lever fast enough to get rid of the opposing men. He was not allowed to go outside to play unless his homework was completed and then he would have to call me at work to get the go-ahead. At night no matter what time I got home I checked his homework which was left on the dining table. One night while reviewing his assignment I noticed that the answers he had to some of the problems which I knew he had covered were incorrect. The following morning after he got dressed for school and had his breakfast, I had him redo his homework before he left the house. That was the last time he did his homework in a hurry.

Once he had a school assignment and was unable to obtain the information from the reference books that were at home. He was becoming extremely irritable. I suggested to him that we go to the library to see what information we could derive there. We located two reference books with similar information. From the assignment we decided on the topics to be covered and who would be responsible for certain ones. Upon completion of our research being satisfied that the relevant areas were covered, he advised me that he would do the paper at home combining both notes. When he was finished compiling the information I gave it a look over to ensure that all the facts were included.

The assignment was handed in on time. When it was graded and returned to him he came to me grinning. He got an A.

As soon as he was sixteen years old he made two announcements. The first one was that he wanted to obtain his working permit and the second was to get his driver's permit. I started off with the easier of the two the work permit. For his junior and senior years in high school he worked as a part-time cashier for a supermarket.

Like me he was very active in school. He was a member of the school choir in elementary school. At the junior high school he performed in the school band and was a member of the school's basketball team. In high school he did track and field and was a member of the National Honor Society.

I taught him how to drive on a five speed manual transmission Toyota Corolla motor car. He picked it up very quickly, adjusting to the use of the clutch in moving off and changing gears. Of course we had our anxious moments: such as him stalling the car in traffic and rolling back when moving off from a grade at a traffic light. Other than that teaching him to drive was not a major issue because he was very anxious to drive.

When I was teaching him to drive I never took him on a mountainous roadway. One day when I was taking him back to college I took a mountainous route and had him drive. I never used the brake in the passenger seat as much as I did that day. He was travelling much faster than I anticipated and he looked very relaxed. I advised him that we were not in any hurry so he should slow down which he did very briefly. When we got to his school I commended him on how well he handled the car over the mountains. He just calmly looked at me and said he learnt it by observing me when I drove. I reflected on what I used to put my Father through when I had an "L" on the car when I was learning to drive. In Jamaica at that time, whenever a student driver was at the controls, a card with the letter "L" in red on a white background was prominently displayed on the front and back of the vehicle.

Challenges And Rewards- Growing Up In A Large Family

As many of you may know growing up in a large family can be very challenging but it can also be very rewarding. It brought us closer together because sometimes there was not much to go around for all of us; so we were taught by our parents to share. We did not have to go looking for playmates because we had each other. We were also taught to look out for each other. But you always have that special sibling whom you confide in, the one you can relate to and you know that he/she will have your back and you will reciprocate. So it was between Pat and me. We looked alike and sounded alike, but that was where the similarities ended because I was even-keeled whereas he was more high-strung. If we were talking behind closed doors, not even my mother could tell us apart sometimes.

Our closeness started just after I left high school. He was the "mail-man" between my high school sweetheart and me, a job that he executed discreetly. Our closeness was further cemented when he was pursuing advanced courses in high school to prepare him for entry to the university. There were no teachers available to lecture for one of the classes he needed as a prerequisite. My mother arranged to have him transferred to a school in Kingston where the course was taught. I was already in Kingston attending classes at a college on a scholarship from my employer.

When he transferred to his new school, we rented a one-bedroom semi furnished apartment. It contained a double bed, a dresser and a dining table with two chairs. There was no stove nor did it have a refrigerator. Luckily, I had won a three-burner gas range from a raffle a few months earlier; so it came in very handy for cooking our meals.

We used to cook two days of the week on Mondays and Wednesdays. On Monday evenings we bought enough meat to last us until Tuesday and again on Wednesdays we purchased enough meat to serve until Thursday. We would go home after school on Fridays and return on Sunday nights. Every evening, we would purchase a bag of ice to keep what little food we had cool. We seldom used the bed at the same time because our study patterns were different. He would study right after we had dinner while I went to bed. I would let him know when he should wake me for my studies. He would then retire for the night and it would be my responsibility to arouse him next day.

He was driving us home one Friday evening. Just as he changed the car into a lower gear to ascend a hill the gear stick came off in his hand. Of course he started to lose his cool; so I calmly told him there was no need to get upset I would hold the gear stick in place so that he could change gears. The drive home that Friday was very entertaining. Whenever he needed to change gears he would announce it, and I held the lever in place for a smooth transmission.

While he was attending the University he lived on campus and upon his graduation he got a job and went to live on his own.

This brother was a one-of-a-kind. He was carefree and sometimes acted irresponsibly. He had a car in which the gas gauge did not work and he never kept up with ensuring that there was enough gas in the tank to cover the amount of driving he did. One day our father came to Kingston on business. It was customary for the both of us to take him back home in order to keep each other company for the return trip. He volunteered to use his car. I asked him if he was sure had enough gas in the car which he assured me there was, then we proceeded to take our father home. When we got to our parents' house, it was very late in the night. My father suggested that we get some sleep and leave early the following morning. We heeded his advice and went to sleep.

We left our parents' house at about 4:45 for our return journey to Kingston, in order for us to get to our respective homes and prepare to get to our jobs by 8:00am. Everything was fine, until we were about three miles from my house. I felt the car jerk. Turning to my brother I asked if the car was out of gas. He was reluctant to respond so I kept badgering him. Eventually he admitted that the gas tank was empty. What made the condition much worse is that we took a back road that passed through an area haunted by gunmen. I told him that I would not be staying there to wait for help, so we better start pushing the car until we got to a more secure spot. We pushed the car non-stop for about ½ mile in the dark until we arrived at a safe haven just as the day started to break. I had to walk to my house because it was too early to get a bus. Once I got my car and returned to my brother, I found him asleep in his car. I got some containers from the trunk of his car, and proceeded to the nearest gas station to have them filled. I had to wait for about ½ hour for it to open. Returning to the scene we put the petrol in the car, and then we went our separate ways. We needed to get to our respective homes to get dressed for our jobs. Later that day I let him have it.

On another occasion we were taking my son's playpen to our parents' house in St. Mary where he was going to spend some time with them. Since my brother's car had a roomier interior he volunteered to take the baby's things. **And yes, it was the same car with the faulty gas gauge.** We stopped by Peter's house on our way to Mom and Dad and had a few drinks while talking. After bidding him farewell we were on to the last leg of our journey. I dozed off but was awakened by my Pat hissing his teeth. Then I felt the jerk and knew what it was. When we stopped by my Peter, he should have purchased gas but he got caught up with the frolicking there and forgot to refuel the car.

The car ran out of gas by an old aerodrome, one mile from the closest gas station (which was closed for the night), and three miles from our destination. This was about 2:00am. Since we were in familiar territory I suggested that we lock the doors and crack the windows so we could get some sleep. I was awakened by a light piercing my face. When I gathered myself together I realized there were two policemen scrutinizing my brother and myself along with the contents of the car with a high powered flashlight. I explained we were taking my son's playpen to our parents when we ran out of gas. This was about 4:00am. After checking our identifications they left and we went back to sleep.

At day-break we got a ride to the gas station purchased some gas then returned to put it in the car. He then pulled into the gas station and filled the gas tank upon my insistence. When we arrived home our mother said she thought that we were coming the night before. I told her to ask my brother why we could not make it and she took care of the rest.

Talking about someone with a short fuse, I do not think he has an equal. At one time we both worked together on the same shift for the same company. I happened to be supervising the shift he was scheduled for on this particular day. When I went to work the person I was replacing advised me of a special assignment scheduled for my brother. Knowing him as well as I do, I knew that it would not sit very well with him. After punching in he came to the counter to be given his assignment. When I advised him of what he was scheduled to do he just lost it and was very belligerent. He was summoned to the manager's office to try to resolve the issue. The manager was not making any progress with a resolution to the problem and was looking rather dejected. He came over to me and asked if I was sure that he was my brother. I replied, "Yes sir same Mother same Father".

Pat never did the assignment he was scheduled for that day.

Sometimes it takes near tragedy for one to exhibit a hidden quality or strength. One weekend we were all at home to visit our father who was hospitalized. When we visited him at the hospital earlier that day, he said he was glad we all came for the weekend because there was a job he had for us. There was an orange tree in the front of the yard with several rotten branches which he wanted us to remove.

Upon our return home all of us assembled under the tree to assess which branches had to be removed. We decided that we would use a saw to cut away the dead branches. I climbed up into the tree, found a comfortable spot and started to cut off the dead branches. So far all the cut branches had fallen from the tree, but there is an adage that says, "Nothing in life comes easy". And so it was with this next branch that I cut. It got entangled with some other branches and would not fall to the ground. I held on to the tree and leaned to my left to give the branch a heave, and then it happened. My left shoulder

Charles P. Atterbury

became dislocated. I had been having this problem on and off since it first occurred while swimming about two years before.

    I made a sigh as I writhed in pain, with my brothers and sisters telling me to try to hold on and try to descend from the tree cautiously. The next thing I knew was that John leapt up the tree and was beside me in no time. He held me by my waist and told me to release my hold on the tree. With me on his shoulder, he started to descend from the tree. When he reached the last branch on the tree he gradually released me onto a chair into the waiting arms of my other brothers and sisters. I always knew that he was strong, but I never knew that he was this strong.

    When I was back on the ground, my other siblings helped to put my shoulder back into its socket while John completed trimming the tree.

Coming To America

On July 15, 1990 I made the boldest move yet. I emmigrated to the United States of America along with my wife and son. We settled in Rockland County, New York, where we shared living accommodations with my brother Pat and his family for a while. The reason for taking this brave step was the educational opportunities available for all of us if we were permanent residents.

It was very difficult trying to adjust to life in a new country. I soon realized it was quite different from being a visitor on vacation. The first thing that I learned was that the climate was unlike Jamaica which is tropical, where the average temperature ranged from the low 30's in the more hilly areas, to the high 80's or 90's in the lower lying and coastal regions. In Jamaica, there was not much distinction between the seasons and you basically dressed the same all year round. Now I found out that I had to dress differently for each of the four seasons.

The winter was the most difficult to get adjusted to. Initially I did not wear layers under my coat so I was constantly feeling cold. Then I learnt to dress in layers and was surprised at the difference it made. Sometimes I would have so many layers under my coat that I would start to sweat.

The next thing that shocked me was that most people had to work two jobs in order to meet their monthly expenses. There was not much time for family get-togethers in which all would be present, because of the various work schedules. My first job was at a supermarket where I worked nights and week-ends. It was very hard for me to get acclimatized to work on Sundays and nights. I was accustomed to free Sundays and leaving work late at night, not starting my workday when it was already dusk. As time progressed I too had to find a second job.

Shortly after we arrived in the United States my wife and I separated. We eventually got divorced in 1994, and I continued to raise Sheldon with some assistance from my brother and his wife whenever I had to go to work. I remarried in August 1995. This marriage also ended with a divorce in 2010.

Presently I live alone.

Summary

As you can see I had a pretty normal and active life filled with near tragedies, plenty of excitement, fun, challenges and surprises. I had many pranks up my sleeve and enjoyed being independent doing the things that I enjoyed. So you can just imagine the shock I got when I was told that I had PARKINSON'S, and found out that I would no longer be able to do most of the things I was accustomed to do with little or no effort. I was stunned. It was as if a car ran out of gasoline or I had been run over by a truck. I felt as if I was struck by lightning. Me, PARKINSON'S, no way! But it was the reality, and I had to face up to it. Life would never be the same again, **ever.** I would have to change my whole lifestyle, and make adjustments as things were becoming more difficult to do, and it was taking me twice as long to achieve the same tasks.

A Visit To My Doctor

There is an adage in Jamaica that states: "you are always all right until you see the doctor". The same can be said about the way I found out that I was stricken with this neurological disorder called PARKINSON'S DISEASE or PARKINSON'S.

What prompted me to visit my primary care doctor was that my brother Peter, who was visiting from the home country, observed that I was not swinging my arms while I was walking and my gait was a bit funny. He mentioned this to my other brother Pat who encouraged me to get it checked out because it seemed unusual. You know how men are when it comes to visiting doctors. I kept putting off making the appointment. Every time my brother asked if I had spoken to the doctor yet I had a different excuse to give him.

I kept procrastinating.

Now this brother can be very persistent. He was like a thorn in my side. He would not relent and kept on pestering me until I succumbed to his pressure of making the appointment with the doctor's office. At first I was a bit hesitant to make the appointment for fear of hearing the worst. Nonetheless I braved it up and called my primary care doctor then made the necessary arrangements to see him as early as possible. The date was finally set and I advised by brother so that he would get off my case.

At my appointment I was very nervous not knowing what to expect because I had seldom been to a doctor before. I had been in the hospital on two previous occasions. The first time was as a result of a car accident and the second time was to repair my left shoulder for a recurring dislocation. After obtaining my medical history it was now time for my examination. The doctor did a complete physical, since I was unable to tell the last time I had one taken. With the physical examination completed he ran some other tests. At the conclusion he wrote a prescription for me to obtain an MRI of the brain and bring the results back to him. He cautioned me that this should be done as soon as possible. It did not dawn on me then to ask why I needed an MRI of the brain.

Obeying the doctor's orders I made an appointment with a diagnostic center for the earliest appointment they had.

Experience At The Diagnostic Center

On the day I went for my MRI I found out that I would be in for a rude awakening and a life changing experience. The test had to be done in a tunnel since this facility did not have the option for an open MRI. The technician explained that it was only a twenty minute procedure. I had to lie still, he would be talking to me, and there was a panic button for me to use any time that I felt uncomfortable in the machine.

After much coaxing and some reassurance from the technician, I agreed for them to proceed with the test. I was placed on a table and inserted into the machine. As soon as the table was in place, the technician announced through a microphone that I should lie still and try not to move my head. A feeling of claustrophobia set in; it was like lying in a coffin with no place to move your arms. At one point during the examination I felt like pressing the panic button just to get out. It was the longest twenty minutes of my life. It was as if I was buried alive.

I tried to calm my fear of being so confined by reflecting on some of the funny experiences I had been through and how I had overcome them. No sooner than my mind was off my confinement, the technician announced that the test was completed and I would be removed from the machine shortly. When I was finally ejected I breathed a sigh of relief. The technician had to have the last word by saying that it was not all that bad. He then told me when to return for the results so I could take them to my doctor.

In about two days I picked up the results of my MRI and made another appointment with my doctor for him to review the results with me. On my return visit I presented him with the pictures of my brain. I saw him examining the pictures more than once and then he knit his brow. I became concerned thinking that there must be something seriously wrong. After mustering up the courage I asked him what was wrong. He did not immediately respond; rather he examined the pictures one last time then he faced me. He said that he thought I was a little young to have what he was thinking. This was in 1998, and I was only 44 years old. He said *I think you have the early stages of PARKINSON'S, but I would like you to make an appointment with a neurologist to be absolutely sure.* He referred me to a neurologist that he knew and instructed me to have him send him a copy of his findings.

This doctor operated from Rockland Neurological Associates. I called his office and made an appointment for the earliest available time. He advised me to take the results of the MRI on the day of my appointment.

Treatment At Rockland Neurological

On the day of my appointment I was armed with the result of my MRI. I was now prepared to meet with the neurologist. He performed the usual gathering of medical history and routine tests that doctors do when you visit them for the first time. In addition, he checked my balance and then my gait. He then examined the MRI and after scrutinizing it for several minutes he concluded that the findings of my primary care doctor were correct. On this visit to the doctor I was accompanied by my wife.

After the examination he sat down with the both of us and explained that I had the early stage symptoms of PARKINSON'S. He explained that it was a life-altering sickness and I would have to make adjustments to my daily routine. I would notice that I would be unable to perform some of the simple things I used to do which I had taken for granted. My speech and posture would be affected as well as my gait.

He then told us that there was no cure for the disease, but he was going to prescribe medication for me to take to help control the PARKINSON'S symptoms, and I should fill it as early as possible. With that being done he advised me to make an appointment to see him again in ninety days.

On my return home I logged onto the Internet and researched PARKINSON'S to find out what caused it, what were the symptoms to look for and what treatments were available. Prior to my diagnosis I had never heard much about this ailment. I was hoping that the doctors' prognoses would be wrong, but the more I read the more convinced I was that the doctors were right. In a nutshell,

PARKINSON's is a brain disorder that affects body movement and motor skills because the area of the brain which produces the chemical *dopamine,* for stimulating such activities is damaged. The early symptoms of PARKINSON'S can be recognized by the twitching of the fingers, displaying what appears to be a masked face, rigidity in movement, stiffness while walking, sometimes freezing in your step or when going through doors. Other symptoms include a slurry speech, an inaudible voice, a poor posture and generally moving slowly.

I was not aware that that I had been displaying some of these early symptoms. My wife would ask me why I was shaking so much and my response to her was that it ran in the family, because my Mother used to tremble a lot a condition we called nervousness. Then I recalled that one day after I made an announcement over the intercom at work a coworker approached me and asked me why I mumble so much whenever I speak. My response to that observation was that I speak very fast or maybe because of my accent so next time I'll make a more conscious effort to speak slowly. On another occasion I was going to check something for a customer when the manager passed me and said that in his store things are done quickly referring to my pace. People used to pass me when I was walking and I would think to myself that they were in a mighty hurry, it took a lot of effort to try to keep pace with them. All along I displayed most of the symptoms but since I was working two jobs and going to school part-time, I simply cast it aside as me being tired and did not for a moment think that something might be physically wrong with me.

All during this time I was working full-time, had a part-time job and pursuing a college degree in accounting. My son had also just started attending the University of Connecticut. Each time that he went to school or had to come home during school breaks, I had to make the trip which was about 140 miles one way. Most of this driving took place late at night after leaving work at 11:00pm. He always drove one leg of the trip to give me a break. I remember jostling with my thoughts about how I was going to let him know that I was diagnosed with PARKINSON'S and also what his reaction would be like. This was the spring semester of 1999. At the end of the semester when I picked him up from school, I told him about my condition during our 2½ hour journey home. Surprisingly, although it came as a shock to him, he took the news fairly well and was very encouraging.

Over a period of time I disclosed to the rest of my family and close friends that I had PARKINSONS. They accepted it with much trepidation, and were interested to know how I was coping with it.

As time progressed, it became increasingly more difficult to perform routine functions such as buttoning the uppermost button of my shirt; brushing my teeth; cleaning my shoes; writing; holding things steadily without them falling to the ground. Even ironing my shirt seemed like such an insurmountable task.

This led to frustration because it was taking me twice as long to do most things. I used to be so independent, and now my whole world appeared to be collapsing around me. Whenever I was home, I would lock myself in my room almost to the point of being a recluse. I did not want anybody bothering me. I just wanted to be left alone. **I WAS DEPRESSED** and did not realize it.

On my follow-up visit to the neurologist, he again tested my balance, and checked my gait. He was not satisfied with the development of my progress with the medication, but he did not change the dosage and advised me to return again in ninety days.

All along I was still active on my job while trying to disguise the symptoms of my illness. I used to hide to take my medication which I kept in my briefcase in an office because I worked on the floor in customer service. If you know anything about customer service then you can imagine how difficult it is to break away from a needy and demanding customer, hence I was not taking the medication on time.

When the neurologist discovered that I was not taking my medication as scheduled, he suggested I keep the pills my pocket for easier access. He was still not satisfied with my progress, so he increased the dosage and told me to see him again in three months.

In the meantime things were getting even more unbearable at home, as each day I was presented with new challenges forcing me into deeper depression. My wife suggested that I make an appointment to see a psychiatrist. Hearing that word I told myself that I was not crazy so I did not need to see a shrink and refused to call one. I would not even give the idea any thought.

At my next scheduled visit to my primary care doctor, he must have recognized my depression. He suggested that I speak with a psychiatrist and, as usual, had one that he referred me to. Reluctantly I made the appointment because I was convinced that only crazy people needed a shrink. Where I'm from there is a certain stigma is associated with people who visit a shrink and it was only my pride that I was fighting with, fearing that I would be seen by someone who knows me and would think that I was "off my rockers "or "going cuckoo". I could not let anybody think I was crazy.

When I went to the appointment my wife joined me. It did not go so well because we disagreed on just about everything. I then concluded that it was a waste of time. For my next session I went by myself.

My neurologist was still dissatisfied with my progress and my reaction to the medication he prescribed. He added a new prescription and had me taking two tablets now instead of one. Again he tested my gait and my balance. He cautioned me that if I had any adverse reaction to any of the pills I was not to hesitate to call him.

I have learned over time that having a supportive family or someone that you can rely on is very important. The reason is that you tend to feel frustrated and give up because you are unable to do some of the things that once posed little or no problems. This puts you in such a depressive state that you just want to be left alone. You get offended at any suggestion to get help doing the things that are now difficult to perform or achieve. I remember a letter fell to the ground one day when I cleared the mail box at home. I had such a problem trying to pick it up I did not realize I had an observer. One of my neighbor's sons came to my aid and picked up the letter for me.

On my job I still did not want anybody to know that I had been afflicted with this disease, fearing that if they knew my employment would be in jeopardy. One day my supervisor approached me to find out what was wrong with me. Of course I was in denial and told her everything was all right. She did not accept that response and insisted that I let her know what the matter with me was, because I was shaking a lot. By this time I was unaware that my symptoms were that noticeable to everybody. I thought I could continue disguising them. Obviously I was not doing a good job of it. She allayed my fears by informing me that if I was thinking my employment would be terminated due to my condition I was making a mistake. So I opened up and told her everything. What also motivated me to open up and discuss my medical condition with more people was that one day while visiting my neurologist at Rockland Neurology I bumped into a fellow worker. Of course, we were both surprised at seeing each other and discussed our reasons for being there.

I had been visiting this neurologist for about two years when he dropped a bombshell. He advised me that he would be retiring at the end of the year so I would have to make my next appointment with a different doctor. I felt numb because I had just started to trust his judgment and felt very comfortable with his patient care for me. I asked him to recommend one. Being the professional that he was, he told me they were all good so I could choose any one of them. He did not commit himself. I randomly selected one whose choice I would not regret.

During my first consultation with my new neurologist, he performed the usual examinations that doctors do for patients they are seeing for the first time, reviewed the notes in my chart recorded by the previous doctor, checked my balance and observed my gait. He reviewed the medications that I was presently taking, and then decided not to change them or modify the existing dosage. He told me to make an appointment to see him in three months' time.

Back on the job I was more open to discussing my medical condition with co-workers and customers alike. I started to take my tablets in the open without thinking what people might be saying. I just did not care anymore.

I had stopped going to public places or where there was a large gathering of people because I would just sweat profusely. At that time I was unaware that it was one of the side effects of the medications. The main anti-PARKINSON'S drug prevents you from stiffening up but it causes a lot of involuntary muscle movements referred to in medical terminology as *dyskinesia*. It's as though you were exercising, hence the sweating. I remember attending a dinner with my wife when I suddenly started to sweat because of the dyskinesia and the room being a little hot. She kept asking me if I took my medication. I kept telling her that it was the medication that was causing me to sweat. Other people at the table kept asking the same question about me taking my medication. I felt that I was a distraction and was causing my wife to be embarrassed, so I excused myself from the table and waited for her outside. There was another occasion when I was attending Church services when I suddenly started to sweat profusely. Members of the congregation came over to see if I was ok and had me sit in front of a fan to cool myself. From that day I tried not to go anywhere there was a gathering of many people in confined places. As funny as it may sound I never had this problem at work or at school.

At school, I was finding it increasingly difficult to take notes in class because my fingers were not moving as fast as I wanted them to. Sometimes it was as if they were frozen, so I had a lot of half sentences throughout my notebooks that were understood only by me. I tried using letters with numerals to substitute for writing out the word. For example, I would write b4 instead of the word "before".

Driving had become a challenge sometimes especially when the medication were wearing off because I would get very stiff. It was as if I was fighting with the car to maintain control of it.

I kept my scheduled appointments with the neurologist. He kept varying the times for me to take the medicines to correspond with the times I felt their effectiveness wearing off.

After seeing the neurologist for about 2 years, my symptoms were getting progressively worse so he increased the strength of one of my medications and prescribed a new one. This resulted in increased dyskinesia. Still I was determined not to let this disease get the better of me. I completed my Associate's degree in accounting in May 2000, at the Rockland Community College in Suffern, New York; attended my son's graduation from the University of Connecticut In May 2002, and graduated from Ramapo College in Mahwah, New Jersey, with a BS in accounting in May 2004.

In my seventh year with Rockland Neurology, my neurologist advised me that he had done all he could with the medicines at his disposal and could do no more to help me; so he was referring me to a neurologist at Columbia Presbyterian Hospital for a second opinion. He advised me that the doctors there had the most up-to-date information on the treatment of people suffering from PARKINSON'S. He further advised that after visiting with the doctor I should return to him for an evaluation.

My wife accompanied me to the neurologist at Columbia. After reviewing the notes from Rockland Neurology, the doctor began to examine me. With what had now become routine with my neurological visits she checked my balance and my gait. She then checked the dosage of the tablets I was taking and although she was dissatisfied with the strength of one of them, she did not recommend any changes.

At some point during the interview with the doctor, my wife and I got into a dispute in which we were in disagreement with most of what was being said, just like our previous visit to the psychiatrist. Shortly afterward my session ended. I was told that a report would be forwarded to my doctor at Rockland Neurological and he would get in touch with me to discuss her findings.

About two weeks later I was called by my doctor's office at Rockland Neurology and an appointment was made to review the outcome of my visit to Columbia. My wife accompanied me. At some point during the evaluation my wife challenged the doctor as to whether I really had PARKINSON'S because she knew of someone else with the disease and the symptoms were different. He explained that the symptoms are generally different from one person to the other and that there are different stages to the disease. Before our session was ended the doctor advised me that he would no longer be treating me. My files would be copied and forwarded to the neurologist at Columbia since they were better equipped to help me further and I should make all future appointments with that facility.

After this session my wife suggested that I have my son take me for my future appointments because it involved driving outside Rockland.

Treatment At Columbia

This next step in my quest to get relief from some of the symptoms of the disease was a major one. It entailed driving to New York City to see my new doctor about thirty miles from home. At this point the dyskinesia was so bad my neck would hurt me sometimes. I called the hospital and made my first appointment as a regular patient of the facility.

For this appointment I visited the doctor by myself. She conducted the routine examinations and of course she checked both my gait and my balance. She then reviewed my medication and was not happy with the strength of one of the tablets I was taking. She wrote a new prescription for tablets at a lower strength. During the session she found out that I was not taking the tablets on time and suggested that I get a pill timer to remind me when it is time to take my medication. The doctor asked about my living conditions and learned that I worked during the days while my wife worked the evening shift and my son was living on his own. She then asked of me what I did when I'm home alone. I told her that I read books, do crossword puzzles, or watched TV. On the matter of family relations she was curious if I had a brother or sister that I could talk and relate with. I informed her that I have a brother who lived in Connecticut. She was very curious about how often we saw each other. When I mentioned to her the infrequency due to our job schedules she suggested we make compromises. She then asked about my eating habits. I was very frank when I told her sometimes I did not feel like eating. Somehow I must have felt sorry for myself and started to cry. When I regained my composure she asked me if I had sleeping problems. I informed her that I sometimes go to bed and sleep for about two hours then get up during the night and have difficulties falling back to sleep.

Then she hit the big one. What was the relationship like with my wife? I advised her that we do not say much to each other because it always ends up in a big fuss.

At this time I did not realize that she was asking these questions to check the level of my state of depression for other future plans she had in store for me. This will be revealed later on.

She ended the session and told me to return in six months.

Sheldon my son accompanied me on my next visit. The doctor reviewed the topics that were discussed during the previous visit. Before we left this session she prepared a list of the things that needed immediate attention, charging Sheldon with the responsibility to ensure that they were executed a job that he did very well. My next scheduled appointment was scheduled for six months later.

Sheldon stepped up to the plate. Firstly, at the appointment desk he changed the telephone contact from my number to his so he would be the first to be called in case there were any appointment changes. This would allow him to arrange the necessary time off from his job. Next step he insisted that I visit my brother because he was going to take me there. By this stage of my illness I had given up on long distance driving. During the weekdays he would randomly check up on me to ensure that I had something to eat. He prepared Sunday dinners so we could both eat together.

All along my primary care doctor was monitoring my progress unknown to me. On my next scheduled visit to him he must have felt very sorry for me the way that I was shaking so much. After my examination he asked me if I had ever thought of having surgery and urged me to think about it. This was now 2006.

During all this time I was still driving to and from work a commute of approximately twenty miles each way. At this stage the shaking had become so bad it was very noticeable, so much so that one day a customer was looking for me but did not know my name. In describing me to a fellow worker she said, the man that is always shaking. My speech was also deteriorating. Many times I had to repeat what I said either because it was inaudible or I could not be understood due to my mumbled speech. My handwriting was now so atrocious that sometimes even I had a difficult time translating it. While using the computer at work I sometimes used both hands to steady the mouse. Things kept falling out of my hands and I was having difficulty grasping or picking them up.

During my next scheduled neurological appointment, the doctor was satisfied with our progress made from the list she'd given us at the previous session. At this appointment I was shaking so out of control my doctor mused that I was doing my aerobic exercises. She decided to eliminate the drug that she had previously reduced the strength on. You could see her look of concern for me. She advised me that she was considering brain surgery at this time because the drugs were no longer helping me. There was one concern she had my lack of stability at home. Somehow she detected some friction between my wife and me when we first visited with her. As she went on to explain, I should have a stable home environment for them to perform such a major brain operation and I would definitely need one after the surgery. She further informed me that I would have to obtain a psychiatric evaluation stating that I was mentally competent before they proceed. By this time I had overcome my resistance about what other people might think if I was seeking help from a psychiatrist. I was prepared to do anything that would provide me relief from the shaking.

Our session concluded with her advising me to see a psychiatrist as early as possible.

My next regular routine visit was due with my primary care doctor the following week. During the consultation he enquired if I had given any thought to his suggestion about the brain surgery. I told him that I was strongly considering it. I brought up my discussions with the neurologist about possible brain surgery and my need to see a psychiatrist. As usual he had one he referred me to. When I went home I called the psychiatrist's office and made the appointment.

At my first meeting with him, I emphasized the importance of seeing him and that he should submit a report to Columbia Hospital after each session. I had three sessions with him before my next neurological appointment was due.

Charles P. Atterbury

At my next neurological session I would learn that the psychiatrist had not furnished any of the reports from our meetings. My doctor excused herself from the room and returned shortly thereafter with another doctor who I later learned had to sign off on all surgeries of this nature. I was hoping to have the DEEP BRAIN STIMULATOR (DBS) operation. With this operation the doctors would drill two holes on either side of my head and insert an electrode into each hole, which would be implanted deep in my brain. The wires would run behind my ears and be attached to two generators which would be inserted into my chest below the shoulder blades. My doctor explained that I met the qualifications for the surgery except that she had not received the psychiatric evaluation. She told him I was very uncomfortable and that they should proceed with making the necessary arrangements as quickly as possible to make the surgery a reality. She was convinced that I would have my son's support. All of this was taking place in May 2007. I was given the neurosurgeon's name and office number and advised to schedule an appointment to meet with him.

I met with my primary care doctor who encouraged me to have the surgery because I was still young and had nothing to lose. He told me about one of his patients who had recently had the same type of surgery and gave me his telephone number. The patient had advised him that he could share his phone number with anyone who needed motivation to undergo the surgery.

When I went home I called this gentleman. You could hear the excitement in his voice when I asked him if he would share his experience with me. A date was set for our meeting over lunch.

On the day that we were scheduled to meet, I picked him up at his house and we went to a diner. From what I could see he was not shaking. During our meeting he strongly urged me to have the surgery, because he had been shaking worse than I was and he was much older. I asked him if he noticed any significant changes after the surgery to which his response was he thought that his voice got lower and he only had a slight tremor in one hand. On the subject of medication he said he was taking one fewer tablet per day. He told me that he no longer did any driving. I asked him how long after surgery it had taken him for a full recovery and he said it was about six weeks. He advised me that he was able to fly on a plane, something he had not done in a long time. When our meeting was over I was more convinced that I would be having the surgery to ease the discomfort of my dyskinesias. I took him back home and promised that I'd keep in touch with him.

The following day I made an appointment with the neurosurgeon for my son and me, so he could advise us on the procedure that the operation would take.

On the day of my appointment, the doctor asked me if I knew of anybody who had this type of surgery performed on them. I told him about my luncheon. He explained that the surgery would be performed in two stages. For the first surgery my head would be bolted to a table to keep it steady. I would be given anesthesia in which the surgeons could talk to me and I would respond, but not be aware of it, while they would plot the path for the wires to be inserted in my brain. Two nickel-sized holes would be pierced in my head. The wires would then be inserted through these holes and they would run behind my ears and into my chest. I would go home for one week and return for the second part in which two pockets would be made in my chest to insert the batteries. The wires that were implanted in my brain the previous week would then be connected to them.

After he was through with his presentation, he asked me if I still wanted to go through with the procedure and I gave him a resounding "YES, DOC". At this point I would do anything to stop the shaking. He turned to my son and asked him what his opinion was. He responded that he was not sure about it but if Dad wants to do it he'll go along with my wishes. He was cautiously optimistic.

Satisfied that we understood what the surgery entailed, he advised us that in a few days we would get a letter from his office outlining pre-operational requirements. Up to this point I had not mentioned anything about the surgery to my wife, because I thought that she was not interested.

I received the letter from the neurosurgeon at the end of June 2007. The first stage of my surgery was scheduled for July 30, 2007, and the second stage was to follow on August 9, 2007. During the two weeks preceding the first surgery I had to undergo the following tests and procedures;

Neuropsychological testing

This test was done to measure my memory, concentration, visual spatial, problem solving, and counting and language skills. Among the tests I was given which was timed, I had to count backwards by seven from the number one hundred to the number one. I was also shown several pictures for a few minutes, and then asked questions about what I could recall from each scene.

Motor-physiology testing

For this test I had to make spirals which were measured by a computer to determine my upper limb motor function. It also included an analysis of my tremor, my reaction time and my movement time.

Blood work

To check if there were any abnormalities in my system.

EKG

This was done to check my heartbeat and to ensure that it was capable of dealing with the stress of the surgery.

MRI of the brain

A picture was taken of my brain.

Pre surgical screening/counseling with a registered nurse

I met with an anesthesiologist, who explained that I would be put to sleep while the doctors operated on my brain. They would be talking to me while inserting the wires in my brain, to make sure they were going in the right path and I would not be aware of any of this. I was also asked if I had any allergic reaction to eggs. The nurse explained that after the second surgery, which was the insertion of the batteries into my chest, I would have to come back to the hospital in order for them to turn them on and program them to my responses to the electrical shocks that I would be feeling.

These tests were completed as scheduled. Now all I had to do was patiently wait for the day of my first surgery.

On the day preceding the surgery the hospital called me at home, advising me to come in for admission by midnight because my surgery was scheduled for 6:00am the following day. By this time my wife heard about the surgery and was upset that I did not discuss it with her. I let her know that I did not see her showing any interest in my doctor's visits and that she showed very little concern about my feelings.

My son took me to the hospital and my wife came along. After my admission he returned home so he could get some rest to be back before I was taken to the operating room at 6:00 the following morning. My wife slept at the hospital so she would be there on time before I was taken in for surgery.

Brain Surgery

On July 30, 2007 my day started at about 5:30 in the morning. I was awakened by the medical staff that wheeled me down to the pre-operating room where I was to be prepared for surgery. My wife and son had been there to wish me good luck. My head was shaved at the two locations where the doctors would make the incisions for the insertion of the wires. I was then wheeled into the operating theater. The last thing I can recall is the surgical team fitting a clamp around my head bolting it to a table and asking me if I was comfortable.

For a surgery which normally takes about eight hours mine was a marathon. It took the surgeons approximately THIRTEEN hours to complete the operation. Yes, you heard right. The doctors told me the reason it took so long is that they had to spend more time in plotting the wires to the correct spot in my brain.

When I was finally out of the anesthesia in the recovery room I was looking into the anxious eyes of my wife, my son and his girlfriend, and Buck (remember him, one of my best friends). I was feeling so famished I told one of the nurses on duty that I needed some food. This comment engendered some laughter among my small group of observers who were wondering if I was OK. Buck jokingly commented that I must be OK, because it did not appear that I had not lost my appetite. I was still feeling ravenous and once more asked for something to eat. I was informed that I should wait for a few minutes because I had just come from the operating theater and if I was given food too early after the surgery it may not settle and would cause me to possibly have an upset stomach leading to problems.

The food finally came and I was consuming it like a ravenous dog so I had to be told to slow down and take it easy.

After the medical staff was satisfied that everything was alright I was assigned a room for overnight observations. I was in no form of pain and the only evidence that I had brain surgery was that my head was bandaged covering the staples that were used to fuse the incision from the operation.

On the morning after my brain surgery a physical therapist visited me to check if I was able to walk without support, wash my face, brush my teeth, or use the toilet without any assistance.

I was discharged from the hospital two days later after the doctor on duty gave me the go-ahead to return home. I was not allowed to lift or bend or drive within the next two to four weeks. At home I carried on business as usual until it was time for my second surgery which would be treated as an outpatient operation.

On August 12, 2007 I received a call from the hospital advising me to report for the second part of my surgery the following morning in the out-patient section by 7:00.

I was taken to the hospital by Sheldon and accompanied by my wife. While I was in the waiting room two of my brothers, Peter and Pat and one of my sisters, Beth, came in to wish me well. Shortly after this meeting, I was taken in by the medical staff to prepare me for the second part of my surgery, placing the two generators into my chest.

The surgery went according to schedule and I was out of the operating room by 4:00pm. I was kept in the hospital for overnight observations. There was no pain from the incisions. The following day I was discharged from the hospital after I was seen by the doctor on duty. At the time I was leaving the nurse on duty asked a porter to take me downstairs in a wheelchair. Once more my pride took control of me. I refused the offer of the wheelchair telling them I was not handicapped and had to be persuaded to use it. Reluctantly I got into the wheelchair and was taken downstairs to wait for the car that was to take me home.

After The Surgery

When I returned home I was expecting to feel pain in the areas where the incisions were made but there was none. I was able to do most of the things that I formerly did. I was still taking my medications but I realized that I could take one fewer tablet for the day. In my opinion I was not shaking as badly as I used to before the surgery.

My next appointment with the neurosurgeon was the following Tuesday when he would remove the staples from my head and as I later learnt, to turn on and program the generators that were placed into my chest during my second surgery. For this appointment I was advised not to take any of my medications.

Sheldon took me for my scheduled appointment. The surgeon was very impressed with my recovery rate and he expressed to me that I did not look anywhere close to what I had been prior to the surgery. After examining me he advised that he was going to remove the staples from my head as I had healed satisfactorily where the incisions were made. I was further informed that he was going to turn on the generators. At this point I expressed surprise because all along I was under the illusion that they were turned on immediately after they were placed into my chest.

After removing the staples from my head the doctor told me to have a seat. It was now time for me to be **switched on.**

When I was comfortably seated he placed a gadget over the generator which was implanted on the right side of my chest. He then touched a button and I immediately felt an electrical shock on my left side. It felt like I was being electrocuted or coming in contact with a high tension electrical wire. Waiting patiently for me to settle after that awakening, he explained that the brain controlled the opposite sides of the body and that was the reason I felt the electrical surge on my left side when he turned on the generator on my right side. He then *tuned* me up according to my responses to his settings. After I was comfortable with the settings he turned on the left generator. This time I was more prepared for the electrical surge through my right side. Here again he *fine tuned* me.

On completion of my *tune-up*, he presented me with a gadget and explained to me that it turns on/off the generators and to check if they are on. It also tests the strength of the batteries. He further advised that it was optional; I could turn them off at nights to extend the battery life or leave them on so that I do not forget to turn them on the following day. In my case it did not matter if I left them on or turned them off because I had a very low setting on the batteries.

The doctor also presented me with a card the size of a credit card and advised to always have it in my wallet to present to security personnel if I am required to go through electronic scanners. That's because the batteries will cause the machine to go off or the magnet might turn off my generators.

When the doctor was finished with me I was told to take my medications. I tried rising from my seat but my legs felt wobbly. I had to lean on the chair for support. The doctor explained that it was normal and that I should relax for a few minutes, so I returned to my seat. The doctor advised me that it would take some time to get adjusted to the batteries and I should give it a few days. If I was not feeling better after about a week I was to call his office and schedule an appointment so that he could re-examine the battery settings. With that I left his office for the day.

Convalescence

Sheldon drove me to my brother Pat in Connecticut. Peter and Beth were also visiting during their vacation and were already there with Pat. In a way I was forced to spend my period of recovery with my brother and his family due to the negative vibes I was getting from my wife at home. She apparently thought that I would be a burden to her and that she would have to take time off from her job to take care of me. As it turned out I was completely independent and did not rely too much on anybody to do anything for me. The only thing I avoided during my recovery was driving.

During the ride to Connecticut I was very uncomfortable. Somehow it just felt that my body was not adjusting to the settings of my generators. I was repeatedly shaking and twitching. By the time I arrived at Pat's house there was little change in the way I felt and I was exhausted from all the physicality's that I had to endure. When I got into the house it was very noticeable to everybody that I was not feeling well and I looked tired. I explained to them that the generators were turned on earlier in the day and my body was adjusting to the settings. They suggested that I lie down for a while and if my condition did not improve overnight I should call the doctor the following day. With that settled I retired to bed early that night.

When I woke up the following morning I was feeling a lot better. There was no feeling of being electrocuted and I was not shaking as badly as I did the previous day. For the next five weeks I was to be my brother and his family's guest.

I was very determined to return to work and would do whatever it took to make this a reality. As a part of my regimen for a speedy recovery, at 6:00am daily for the next two weeks Peter and I walked for one mile from my brother's house to the track field at the Manchester

High School. At the school I walked about six laps around the track which was the equivalent of 1½ miles; take a short break, then trek the mile back to his home.

After about six weeks into my recovery period I began to feel extremely bored, sitting around doing nothing but reading and solving crossword puzzles. I called my job and advised them that I was ready to return to work. They instructed me that that I would need a letter from my doctor declaring that I was capable to return to work with no restrictions or limitations.

I contacted the doctor and he provided the letter declaring me medically fit to return to full duty with no restrictions or limitations. A copy was sent to my employers who gave me the approval to return to work. By this time I started to drive again.

Return To Active Duty

And so it was. On Monday October 8, 2007, I returned to work as happy as a lark and full of confidence.

The reaction from the customers and my co-workers was, Wow! I can't believe that it is you. You are no longer shaking and you look so well rested and calm.

I was in awe listening to all their cheers and kind words of encouragement, it really touched me. It was then that I realized how obvious my shaking was. It then hit home to me that the only person I was fooling about trying to hide the symptoms of my sickness was me. Remember the adage *you can fool some people some time, but you can't fool all the people all the time.*

Returning to work after my surgery made me realize how much one is under public scrutiny and how much we are being observed by others. It felt really good to know how my boldness to undertake such a risky surgery was admired by so many people.

After the first day it was back to business as usual. I did observe that my voice was not as powerful as it used to be before I had the surgery and that I had to repeat myself oftentimes until someone understood what I was talking about. I get the impression that people just nod their heads or they pretend to understand what I am saying because they do not want to offend me by asking me to repeat myself. I am well aware of this because I see when their faces get blank after I have spoken.

It is equally frustrating for me too because I know what I am saying but sometimes the words don't always come out right, especially when the medication is wearing off. There have been times when I was in conversations and I would start stuttering before uttering the first word. I am well aware of this problem so sometimes when I am with friends I seldom participate in conversations for fear that I might not be heard or understood.

Living With Parkinson's

As with any chronic disease, Parkinson's is no exception. The sooner you come to grips with the fact and acknowledge that the sickness is not like the common cold or a sprained joint which lasts for a short time and then goes away with or without treatment, the better it will be for you and those closest to you. You have to accept that the condition is irreversible and you will have to live with it until the day you die. What also helps is learning as much as you can about how the disease affects the body and the changes that are to be expected in everyday life. It is very important to have a loving and caring partner one who takes the time to learn and understand the restrictions that you now have to face.

I have learnt firsthand how depressive a chronic illness makes you feel. Just thinking about the things you are no longer able to do with little or no effort because of your current inhibition makes you feel totally incapacitated. It is very hard to acknowledge that you are suffering from depression, because you live in constant denial that there is something wrong with you.

For me personally it was very hard to accept the fact that I would be limited in completing routine tasks and everyday activities. When I was first diagnosed in 1998, I was still carrying on daily tasks with very little difficulty. In fact this was the year that Sheldon started to attend the University of Connecticut and I was very busy driving him back and forth from school. As the disease progressed I soon realized the physical toll it was taking on my body. I would be so relieved to get to his school so he could take over the driving because at times my muscles would get so stiff while driving that it was as if I were having a fight with the car.

Luckily for me this only lasted for two years. When he was to start his junior year I was able to buy him a reliable used car so that he could drive himself to and from school at his own convenience. Then the worrisome part set in. Whenever he was travelling to or from school I would not stop praying for his safe journey until I either heard from or saw him. His right foot was very heavy on the gas pedal.

My biggest driving challenge living with Parkinson's was in the summer of 2000. My ex-wife and I decided to spend a week's vacation with one of her sisters in South Carolina. After comparing the cost of flying, taking the train, or driving it worked out to be much cheaper if we drove; and we would arrive at our destination by train at about the same time as it would take us to drive. When I mentioned this to other members of my family they were very skeptical and thought that the journey would be too strenuous for me. They relented when they saw my determination to do it.

On the day we departed for Florence, South Carolina, we left home at approximately 6:00 am with me being the designated driver. The journey was about 662 miles one way and we did it in about thirteen hours travelling at an average speed of 80 MPH. I drove almost the entire distance except for about one hour when my ex-wife drove while I slept because I had worked the previous night and got home a little after midnight.

I scheduled my stops for refueling, eating, and using the restrooms at the times that my medications were due. Other than these *pit stops* the ride down was incident free. When we arrived in Florence my in-laws were very shocked that we made it down from New York so quickly given my condition with Parkinson's.

On our return journey for home, I did all the driving with more frequent stops.

My typical day starts between 5:00 & 5:30 am. This is when I take my first dose of medication consisting of two tablets. I then return to lie in bed for about half an hour while waiting for the medication to start taking effect by getting my muscles loose. At about 5:30 am I try to have morning devotion for about ten to fifteen minutes. I try to get to the bathroom by 5:45, because gone are the days of taking five to ten minute showers. Now it takes me ten to fifteen minutes or longer depending on how loose the muscles are. Since it takes me twice as long to do things I try to be as proactive as I can. While I am taking my shower the kettle is on the stove on low fire so I can make my cup of *Joe* before going to work. Work commences at 7:30 am, and it is about ten miles from home so I try to leave by 7:15 am.

One of the tablets prescribed for me should be taken at three (3) hour intervals. Sometimes I get so carried away on the job I miss taking it on time, and then when I remember it is when I start stiffening up and crawling. At this point my voice will be very low and my speech muffled. I have discovered that as soon as I take it, if I sit down for about five to ten minutes the medication takes effect, then I'll be good to go until it is time for the next dose.

It is good to work with people who are considerate and understanding. One day I totally forgot to take my medication at 2:00 pm, so as soon as I remembered I took it. Before the tablet took effect the manager saw me barely moving as my gait was shuffling. He enquired if I was ok. I explained to him that I had not taken my medication at the scheduled time so I was now paying for my tardiness. When I was satisfied that it was ok for me to leave for home I proceeded towards my car and just as I opened the driver's door the manager enquired if I would be ok to drive home. I assured him that I was. It took me by surprise because I was completely unaware that he had still been observing me all along.

The rest of my co-workers are equally caring towards me. They get very concerned when they see me struggling to do simple things. If they see me trying to tie my shoe lace someone is always there to assist me. If I lose my balance somebody is available to support me and prevent me from falling.

I like to face challenges. In 2010, I called my brother in Connecticut and told him that I was going to visit him and spend the Memorial weekend at house and that I would be driving alone. His reaction was if I was sure I could handle such a journey all by myself. I told him I was willing to give it a try. We agreed that I should not travel during the night. On the Friday before Memorial Day I left my home in Rockland at about 3:00pm. The distance between our homes is 116 miles and the commuting time is approximately 2 hours under normal driving conditions. The arrangement was that when I was leaving my house I should call him so that he would monitor my travel. I arrived safely at my destination within the prescribed time frame much to the excitement of my brother and his family.

Since then I have spent many holiday weekends with my brother and his family. Each time that I make these trips I make two phone calls before leaving my house. The first is to my son, to let him know my whereabouts, and the other to my brother, advising him that I'm on my way. Upon my arrival at my brother's house I call my son advising him that I have safely got to my destination.

In my mind I think that I can still do the things that I used to do but my body keeps reminding me those times have changed. Little by little I have been conceding that I am limited in the things I can do by myself. In the past when pride used to let me refuse to accept people's offer to assist me to do simple things, I have now resigned myself to accept these offers. I have also learned that the more people I share the nature of my illness with the more they understand why my movements are sometimes slow. I am very surprised by the kindness of people who always seem to be ready to help me once they sense that I am having a problem.

Holding a pen has become extremely difficult for me, but being the stubborn and determined person that I am makes me able to *get a grip*. Other tasks which have become problematic include tying my shoelaces, holding things in my hands for long long periods, bathing, and combing my hair. Any action that requires the use of your fine motor skills poses a challenge but with a lot of self-motivation and perseverance, it can be achievable. I have resigned myself to take things in strides, putting on foot before the other. One step at a time, as my father would say.

There is an old adage **IF YOU CAN'T BEAT THEM JOIN THEM.** I know I have a fighting spirit, but since it is not strong enough to ward off Parkinson's, I use all the aids necessary to help make my day-to-day activities less burdensome. I keep telling myself that I have the disease, the disease does not have me. I can still have a good life, although there will be restrictions and boundaries as to what I can do without hurting myself.

www.ingramcontent.com/pod-product-compliance
Lightning Source LLC
Chambersburg PA
CBHW052203110526
44591CB00012B/2061